Nymph Award for the best film at the Monte Carlo
Television Festival. His other plays include *The Rise and
Fall of Little Voice* (Royal National Theatre, Cottesloe, 1992
and the Aldwych Theatre, London, 1992) winner of the
Evening Standard Best Comedy Award in 1992 and the 1993
Olivier Award for Best Comedy.

by the same author

Road
The Rise and Fall of Little Voice

Jim Cartwright

Two & Bed

METHUEN DRAMA

Methuen Modern Plays

Two & Bed reissued with a new cover as a collection and
published in Great Britain 1994
by Methuen Drama

10 9

Methuen Publishing Limited
215 Vauxhall Bridge Road, London SW1V 1EJ

Peribo Pty Ltd, 58 Beaumont Road,
Maint Kunng-Gai, NSW 2080,
Australia, ACN 002 278 761
(for Australia and New Zealand

Methuen Publishing Limited Reg. No. 3543167

Two was first published as *To* in 1991 by Methuen Drama
and is reprinted here with corrections
Copyright © 1991, 1994 by Jim Cartwright
Bed was first published in 1991 by Methuen Drama
and is reprinted here with corrections
Copyright © 1991, 1994 by Jim Cartwright

The author has asserted his moral rights

ISBN 0–413–68330–3

A CIP catalogue record for this book
is available at the British Library

The photograph on the first cover is from the 1990 Young
Vic production of *Two* (*To*) with John McArdle and Sue
Johnston. Copyright © Gordon Rainsford.

Printed and bound in Great Britain
by Cox & Wyman Ltd, Reading, Berkshire

Papers used by Methuen Publishing Limited
are natural, recyclable products made from wood grown in
sustainable forests. The manufacturing processes conform to
the environmental regulations of the country of origin

Caution

Contents

Two was first performed at the Bolton Octagon on 23 August 1989, with Sue Johnston and John McArdle playing all the characters:

Landlord
Landlady
Old Woman
Moth
Maudie
Old Man
Mrs Iger
Mr Iger
Lesley
Roy
Fred
Alice
Woman
Little Boy

Directed by Andrew Hay
Designed by Mick Bearwish
Lighting by Phil Clarke

Note

The action takes place over one night, in a pub, in the North of England.

Two is designed so that two people can play all the characters. The set consists of a pub bar, with all glasses, pumps, till, optics etc., being mimed as are the other people in the pub to whom the actors relate. There are also instances in the play where members of the audience may be directly related to, if it is appropriate to the production.

The action should flow from one scene to the next without a break, therefore costumes should be minimal.

Two

Blackness. Suddenly, lights up on **Landlord** *and* **Landlady** *behind bar working and serving.*

Landlord There you go love, two pints. Tar.

Landlady What was it now? Babycham and two Appletisers.

Landlord And now sir, a pint and a half of lager.

Landlady It was a Babycham wasn't it?

Landlord (*from mouth corner*) Get it together.

Landlady Sod off. (*To customer.*) There you go dear.

Landlord Thanks. And what's your poison? (*To someone else.*) Be with you in a minute.

Landlady Tar. Nice to see you two back together again. Yes.

Landlord (*while serving*) Er, can you see to this lad here love?

Landlady (*still to customer*) Right lovey, see ya. (*To* **Landlord**.) Eh?

Landlord Here love, customers, thirsty. (*Under breath.*) Move it woman.

Landlady Stuff it man. (*To customer.*) Yes love can I help you?

Landlord Right then, with ice was it?

Landlady Sorry, no cherries.

Landlord (*to* **Landlady**) What's them down there, blind arse.

Landlady You'll have a lager instead, okay. (*To* **Landlord**.) Don't get smart with me Pigoh.

Landlord Uh. There you go now. Thanks.

Landlady (*to someone leaving*) See you. What? Oooooooooh.

Landlord (*glares at her, then to customer*) Nice to see you, what's it to be? White wine and a Barbican.

Landlady Two double Drambuies, well well. Where the hell is that now?

Landlord There! There! (*Realises he's shouting and laughs back at customers. To* **Landlady**.) You'll be the death of me.

Landlady If only, if only.

Landlord Get damn serving.

Landlady I am. I am, if you'll keep your poxy nose out.

Landlord (*to customer*) Oh sorry. What was it again?

Landlady (*she cracks up laughing at this, he gives her a black look. To customer*) Two double Drambuies for you.

Landlord White wine and a Barbican. Not in the same glass I hope, ha!

Landlady (*at joke*) Oh my God. (*Serves customer.*) There you go loves. Tar.

Landlord Love, can you just reach me a Barbican from down there.

Landlady Where? Oh yes.

She crouches down for it. He quickly goes down too. They are both out of view.

Landlady Ow.

Landlord (*comes up*) Here we are.

Landlady (*comes up, rubbing her side*) Little swine. Ow. I'll get you for that. (*To customer at bar.*) Yes. Ah it's the happy couple. What would you like then?

Landlord So that's four Grolshes, two Buds, and a packet of peanuts.

Landlady Two sweet white wines, how nice. You didn't get much of a tan then.

Landlord There you go, your wish is my command.

Landlady There you go, on the house.

Landlord *spins round to glare.*

Landlady Well it was this very pub in which you met, wasn't it? Yes. Lovely, lovely. See you later.

Landlord (*to* **Landlady**) On the house. Lovely. Lovely. (*Suddenly realises couple are waving to him from their table.*) What? Oh congratulations. Awww, our pleasure.

Landlady Creep.

Landlord Crap.

Landlady Fart.

Landlord Hag.

Landlady (*steps over to a customer*) Two whiskeys was it? (*And straight over his foot.*)

Landlord Arrr. Ohh.

Landlady Oh dear, are you all right, love? He wants to take the weight off his feet, I keep telling him. Now then, two whiskeys.

Landlord (*distracted by customer*) A brandy and cider, right you are. Not in the same glass I hope. Ha.

Landlady *cringes.*

Landlady (*taking money*) 2.05 loves. Tar now.

Landlord There's your brandy, we'll soon have the cider beside her.

Landlady Painful. Painful.

Landlord It will be. It will be.

Landlady Sorry? (*Turns towards customer's voice.*) Oh it's you, how are you? I was wondering when you'd pop up.

Landlord 2.50 thanks. Lovely. (*To* **Landlady** *as she passes.*) Don't embarrass us, you look like his grandmum.

Landlady Do you want what you had last night? Oooooooh, you young wag. No serious though, what's your choice love? Okay. Well thanks I will. Thanks very, very much, you gallant young boy.

Landlord A Southern Comfort and crisps. (*He goes to get them.*)

Landlady (*to* **Landlord**'s *customer*) If he says 'Not in the same glass', don't laugh please.

Landlord Not in the same glass, I hope?

Landlady (*laughs, then to her customer*) Now then sparrow, there you go, and tar, tar again. (*She winks.*)

Landlord Get out and get some glasses while it's quietening. Go on.

Landlady I'm going. I'm a going. (*She does.*)

He breathes out. Grabs up a cloth and starts wiping glasses.

Landlord (*turns to audience*) First night in here? Well, you'll get used to us. We're a lively pub. It's calmed down a bit now, but it comes in waves. Not going to ask you what you're doing here, never do, that's one of our few rules. We get a lot of rendezvousers here you see, but we're also strong on couples, don't get me wrong. They either come in pairs or end up that way. That woman over there is my wife, bitch. I run this place virtually on my own. We've been here bloody years. In fact we met outside this pub when we were kids, me and cow. Too young to get in, snotty conked, on tip-toes peeking through the frosted windows. We had our first drink in here, we courted in here, we had our twenty first's in here, we had our wedding reception here, and now we own the bloody place. I only did it for her, it's what she'd always wanted. Done some knocking through recently, got the walls down, made it all into one. You can get around better, and more eyes can meet across a crowded room. Better that, better for business and pleasure and for keeping an eye on that roving tart. Where is she with them glasses? Wouldn't mind a bloody drink meself, I'll have one later. It's a constant battle keeping your throat away from the stock. It

really is the landlord's last temptation. Because this is it
for us proprietors. This is our life, these bar sides, to them
wall sides and that's it. People and pints and measures
and rolling out the bloody barrel. Working and social life
all mixtured, a cocktail you can't get away from. Until
night when we fall knackered to bed. But I'm not
complaining, no, no. As long as many mouths are clacking
at many glasses and the tills keep on a singing. What more
could a publican want?

Old Woman *enters*.

Landlord Oh here she is, I can set the clock by this auld
dear. (*Puts glass under pump ready*.) Evening love, usual?

Old Woman Yes please, landlord.

Landlord How's everything love?

Old Woman Passing same. Passing sames.

Landlord Oh aye. There you go.

Old Woman Thank you, landlord.

Landlord Pleasure lovey. (*He goes*.) Where is she with
them bloody glasses?

He exits. She sips her drink. Then turns to the audience.

Old Woman Here I am at the end of my day. Taking my
reward from the glass. He's at home, he can't come out,
too crippled dear. But he allows me out for my drink at the
end of it all, the day. I've retired, but not really, 'cause
now I have to work twice as hard with him, lifting his
shitty bum off the blankets. He's having all the last bit of
my life, but I don't begrudge him that. Poor lumped man
he is, there he is at home, with his pint of dandelion and
burdock, watching the television in the dark. All's I do is
look after him and shop a lot, shop a lot with nowt.

Though I do like to go shopping, I like to, I like the
butcher best, blood everywhere, laughing his bloody head
off. He's fat too, fat. Fat like jelly pork. Pink. I love him,
though he doesn't know of course. It's his laughing that
does it, and his big butcher life, chopping and pulling
those beasts apart. Admirable. Me, myself, don't have
much strength left now, carrying my husband down the
stairs, I have to stop three times, my arms keep giving.
'Let's have our breather' I say, and we both stop, panting
like knackered cattle. I watch his chest going like the
clappers, and I watch mine going the same. And all our
wheezes echoing off the stairway and my swollen ankles,
and his watery eyes, and I wonder in God's starry heavens
why we keep going. We have each other, we have the
allowance, there's a lot of memories somewhere, there's a
bit of comfort in sleep and Guinness, but what the hell has
it all been about? I ask you. I carry him down. I carry him
up, piss all over my hands. His day, the tele-box. My day,
shopping bag. Butchers for a bit o' scrag, see him flipping
open the animals with his very sharp knife. Oh my day,
my life, my day, my drink here. Him at home with the
tele, in the burdock dark a dead dandelion in his mouth. I
can hear his old chest creaking from here, and on my neck
his chicken arms, chicken arms, and around my neck his
poorly chicken arms. Get me a Guinness. Stand me a
drink. Fetch the butcher with his slaughtering kit, may I
ask you all to raise your cleavers now please and finish the
job, raise them for the bewildered and pig weary couples
that have stuck, stuck it out. Thank you.

She bows her head as though to have it cut off.

Lights pick up **Moth** *chatting a young woman up. Imaginary or
real from the audience. (This scene may be performed in Liverpool
accents if desired.)*

Moth You're beautiful you. You're absolutely beautiful
you. Look at you. You're fantastic you. I love you. I love

the bones of you. I do. You think it's too quick don't you.
But you can't see yourself. You're just . . . I'm in love with
you, I'm not joking. I've seen some women, but you. Let's
get back to what you are, beautiful. Did you just smile
then or did someone turn the lights on? You are beautiful
you. You stand for beauty. You sit for it too. Look how
you sit you, like a glamour model that's how. You . . .
You're quiet though, but I love that in a girl, love that,
don't get me wrong. You're beauty you. Beauty itself.
Beauty is you. You're marvellous as well as being beautiful
too, you. Yes, too good for this place I'll tell you that.
What's a beautiful girl like you doing in a place like this,
or whatever they say, is that what they say, who cares,
who cares now, eh? You are a star, and you don't even
know it. A star before you start. Everything about you's,
just . . . You are it. The beauty of all times. You're just
beautiful and that's it! Done, finished, it. Because you are
the most beautiful thing ever brought to this earth. And
you're for me you. You are for me. There's no bones about
it, none! Here's the back of my hand, here, here. And
here's the pen, number, number please, number, before I
stop breathing.

Maudie *has entered and taps him on the shoulder.*

Maudie Hiyah Moth.

Moth What are you doing here?

Maudie I'm your bleeding bird aren't I?

Moth (*looking round*) Yes, yes, but . . .

Maudie Moth. Moth she wasn't interested.

Moth How do you know that?

Maudie Believe me I know. Moth, Moth do you still love
me?

Moth Of course I do, get them in.

Maudie No, I'm not this time.

Moth Eh?

Maudie I've had a good talking to by some of the girls at work today. And they've told me once and for all. I've not to let you keep using me.

Moth Using. Using. You sing and I'll dance. Ha! No Maudie you know that's not me. But when I'm broke what can I do, I depend on those that say they love me to care for me. And anyway it's always been our way.

Maudie Stop. Stop now. Don't keep turning me over with your tongue.

Moth Maudie, my Maudie.

He takes her in his arms, kisses her. She swoons.

Maudie Oh here get the drinks in.

Moth (*he opens handbag*) Ah that sweet click. (*Takes out some money.*) Here I go.

He sets off around the other side of bar to get served.

Maudie Oh no. No. Look he's off with my money again . . . I said this wouldn't happen again and here it is, happened. I've got to get me some strength. Where is it? (*Makes a fist and twists it.*) Ah there. Hold that Maudie. Maudie, Maudie hold that.

Moth *on his way back with the drinks. Bumps into someone. Dolly bird.*

Moth Oops sorry love. Bumpsadaisy. You all right . . .

Maudie Moth!

Moth See you. Better get these over to me sister. (*Passing others.*) 'Scuse me. (*Others.*) Yep yep. (*Others.*) Beep beep. Here we go Maud.

Maudie What were you . . . (*Shows fist to* **Moth**.)

Moth (*giving drink*) And here's your speciality.

Maudie Aww you always get it just right. Nobody gets it like you. The ice, the umbrella.

Moth Of course. Of course.

Maudie *kisses him.*

Maudie Oh look, I'm going again. All over you.

Moth That's all right, just watch the shirt.

They drink. He begins looking around. She looks at him looking around. She makes the fist again.

Maudie Look at me will you. Look at your eyes, they're everywhere, up every skirt, along every leg, round every bra rim. Why oh why do you keep chasing women!

Moth Oh we're not going to have to go through all this again are we petal. Is this the girls at work priming you?

Maudie Yes a bit, no a bit. I don't know. I can't remember now, so much has been said. I just want you to stop it.

Moth But you know I can't stop myself.

Maudie But you never even get off with them.

Moth I know.

Maudie It's like the girls say, I hold all the cards.

Moth How do you mean?

Maudie I'm the only woman on earth interested in you.

Moth Well yes, but . . .

Maudie Moth let it all go and let's get settled down.

Moth I can't it's something I've always done and I guess I always will. (*Again looking at some women.*)

Maudie No, Moth, no . . . Oh how can I get it through to you.

Moth (*draining his glass empty*) Drink by drink.

Maudie No way. Buzz off Moth.

Moth Come on love, get them in. Let's have a few and forget all this. You pay, I'll order.

Maudie No.

Moth But Maudie, my Maudie.

Maudie No, I'm stopping the tap. I shall not be used.

Moth Used. Used. Well if that's how you feel I can always go you know:

He walks down the bar a bit, stops, looks back, walks down the bar a bit, stops, looks back. Falls over a stool. Picks it up, laughs to cover embarrassment, limps back to her.

Maudie, I've been thinking, all what you're saying's so true and right as always. I'm losing everything, my flair, my waistline, what's next to go – you? Will it be you next?

Maudie (*unmoved*) You'll try anything won't you, just to get into my handbag. The romantic approach, the comic approach, the concern for me approach, the sympathy approach. Does it never end?

Moth You forgot sexy in there.

She swings for him, he ducks.

No Maudie. You're right again. What does a princess like you see in a loser like me?

Maudie I don't know. Well I do. You're romantic, like something on the fade. I love that.

Moth (*moving in*) Oh Maudie, my Maudie.

As he does, she starts to melt again, he starts to reach into her handbag, she suddenly sees this and slams it shut on his hand.

Maudie Stop!

Moth Aw Maud. How can I prove I'm genuine to you? Here take everything on me, everything, everything. (*Starts* *frantically emptying his pockets*.) My last 10p, I'm going to give it to you!

Maudie I don't want your poxy ten.

Moth You say that now, you say that now Maud, but you don't know what it's going to turn into. I'm going to give you all I've got left. My final, last and only possession. (*Spins and drops it in Juke box*.) My dancing talent.

'Kiss' by Tom Jones comes on. **Moth** *dances.*

Moth 'Cause Maud, whatever you say. Whatever's said and done. I'm still a top dancer 'ant I hey?

Maudie Well you can move.

Moth I can Maud. I sure as hell can Maud. (*Dancing*.) I'm dancing for you Maudie. For you only. (*Dancing*.) Come on get up here with me.

She comes to him, puts her handbag on the floor, they dance.

Moth Who's lost it all now eh?

He really grooves it.

Maudie (*worried, embarrassed*) Moth.

Moth Come on doll.

Maudie Moth take it easy.

Moth Come on. Swing it. Let your back bone slip. Yeah let your . . . Awwwwwwwa Ow ow!!! (*Stops. Can't move.*)

Maudie Moth, oh God, what is it?

Moth Me back, me back. Help oh help.

Maudie What can I do! What can I do!

Moth Get me a chair, get me a gin.

Maudie (*feeling up his back*) Where is it? Where is it?

Moth There between the whiskey and the vodka.

Maudie Ooo another trick, you snide, you emperor of snide! (*Hits him.*)

Moth No, no Maud. Really, you've got it all wrong. It's real. Arwwwwww. Get me to a chair!

Maudie It's real is it you swine?

Moth Real. Real.

Maudie Real is it?

Moth (*nodding*) Arrgh. Arrgh.

Maudie Okay let's test it.

Moth How?

She takes out a fiver and holds it in front of him. He tries to go for it, but he can't.

Maudie (*amazed*) It is true. (*Starts circling him.*) Trapped. At last after all these years, I finally have that fluttering Moth pinned down. Ha.

Moth Oh Maudie what you gonna do?

Maudie Let's see. Let's see here.

Moth Don't muck about now. I'm dying here, arrrgh, dying.

Maudie So if, if, I help, what do I get out of it?

Moth Anything! Anything!

Maudie Anything, anything eh?

Moth Yes, yes, arrrrgh.

Maudie Okay, make an honest woman of me now.

Moth No, never, arrrr.

Maudie Okay, see you love.

Moth No. Don't go Maud please.

Maudie Sorry love, have to, love to stay but . . . 'bye. And if any of you try to help him, you'll have me to deal with, and my handbag.

Maudie *blows him a kiss as she goes. Exits.*

Moth MAUD! Will you marry me?

Maudie (*coming back*) Sorry?

Moth Will you marry me?

Maudie YES! OH YESSSSSSSSS! (*She comes running to him and hugs him.*)

Moth (*she's hurt his back*) AARRRRGHHHH!

Maudie Oh sorry love.

Still in embrace she guides him to a stool.

Moth A a aa a.

She props him against stool and bar, he is stiff like a board.

Moth Ah.

Maudie Oh Oh. (*Cuddling him.*) Oh. (*Suddenly serious.*) Do you still mean it?

Moth I mean it. I mean it. Singleness is all over for me.

Maudie (*hugging him again as best she can*) Oh Moth you won't regret this.

Moth Arrgh. I know. I know.

Maudie I'll get us a taxi. Hold on now. Be brave. You poor thing.

She rushes out.

Moth (*turns, as best he can, to girl at front*) You're beautiful you. Look at you. You're fantastic you.

Blackout.

Landlady *enters from where they exited.*

Landlady (*calling back*) Handcuff him Maudie, handcuff him now. (*To audience.*) Look at that Maudie, over the moon and back, she wants to watch herself with that scallywag. Ahh, I enjoy a lull like this, you can get a decent chat in can't you? He hates lulls, if the till's not singing he starts crying. (*Waves to someone.*) All right. (*To someone else.*) Hiyah, I'll try and get over there in a minute. I like that part of pub life, the people. That's why it's a peach in here, so many people pairing up in front of your very eyes, very heart-warming, heart-rending. (*Looks off.*) Look at Pigoh go, the prat. (*Shouts.*) Hey you all right with those crates?

Landlord (*shouts from off*) Course I am. Bugger off!

Big crash is heard.

Landlady *titters.*

Landlord (*off*) OH MY GOD! MY PROFITS!

Landlady I don't know. Without me this place would collapse around the bastard, it really would. I'm the brains behind the operation you might say. He's got no idea really, he knows how to run around, but not how to run a pub. Sad but true, but funny too. You've got to laugh haven't you? This is our life, this public house and all who 'ale' in her. No social life, family life. Work, business, pleasure, all pulled from behind the bar, and beyond that only a loveless bed to lie in. Still, I have my consolations, like sipping away Pigoh's profits, and really, well there's never a dull moment when you deal in liquor. And you get to meet the choicest of people. Like this old love here.

Old Man *enters.*

Landlady How do Pops.

Old Man How do love.

Landlady What you on, a bitter or a stout?

Old Man Mild please.

Landlady Nothing like a change.

Old Man That's right dear.

Landlady You're a lovely old bugger you. Why don't you and me run away together. Just whisk me off me feet, I wouldn't say no.

Old Man Ha Ha.

Landlady Oh well, there you go Pops. (*Gives him drink.*) No, have it on me.

Old Man (*trying to pay*) Nay, here.

Landlady No, my treat.

Old Man Thank you.

Landlady My pleasure. (*Off to serve someone else.*) Yes love. (*Exits.*)

Old Man Howdo. (*Sups beer.*)

Pause.

They all think I'm quiet. (*Sups.*)

Long pause.

But there's a good reason for that.

Pause.

I'm having a very good time within.

Pause.

(*Smiles.*) With my wife. She's dead, but still with me. Not like a ghost or any of that old kak.

Pause.

It's just a feeling. (*Sups.*)

Don't go yet, I'm not mad tha' knows.

Pause.

Sometimes if the feeling's not come of its own
I can generally bring it on
by touching our teapot,
brown pot,
and this'll start something
brewing,
sweet,
present,
soft
as her cotton hair.

Long pause.

Then it deepens. (*Closes his eyes.*)

Pause.

She's here now.

Nice.

She was here when I came in
but it's more better now.

Pause.

It's like . . .

Pause.

Being held.

It's just

comfort of her
without anything else.

Pause.

She's gone now. (*Opens eyes.*) So that's how we come and go to each other during the day. (*Sups.*)

Pause.

And how deep we do soak in each other sometimes. So deep I can hardly stand from the chair. And this is how I think I'll go one day. I'll just tag on and slip off with her when she leaves. And somebody will come round to our house and find my empty shell. (*Chuckles, drinks, rests.*) Life's just passing in and out in't it? Very comfortable, very nice to know that. (*Finishes drink.*) Ta tar. (*Goes.*)

Landlady *enters with sandwich.*

Landlady Cheese and onion! (*To someone close by.*) Keep your eyes off, you. I've done this as a favour for . . . Where is she? (*Sees her, goes to her.*) There you are love, get that down you. (*Takes money.*) Tar. (*To someone else.*) Love the trousers, who'd have thought they'd come back in. Only joking love, very natty them.

Landlord *enters.*

Landlord The queen of tittle tattle.

Landlady Sod off.

Landlord Out of the cellar and into the boxing ring, that's me. (*Hits the bar side, enters bar.*)

Landlady (*also enters bar, puts money in till*) Ting ting, tills away, round bleedin' one.

Landlord Will you back off for once.

Landlady Never.

Landlord (*to customer*) Same again Jack? (*Puts glass up to optics.*)

Landlady (*to her customer*) Just the one pet, sure. (*She reaches up to optics, their arms cross.*)

Landlord What's up with you tonight?

Landlady I think you know.

Landlord (*gives drink, takes money*) Ta mate.

Landlady (*gives drink, takes money*) Thanks love.

They both come back to till and put money in.

Landlord I don't know what you're on about.

Landlady (*she closes till*) Ting ting, round two. Yes you do, yes you do.

Landlord Run a pub.

Landlady (*turns into corner to work*) That's it, turn to the ropes when the jabs get too close.

Landlord (*looks up*) What the bloody hell's this coming in!

Landlady Ting ting, match postponed!

Landlord It's a stag party. Man the pumps, pull out the stops, raise the prices, come on let's polish them off. You take the spirits, I'll take the beers.

Landlady *leaves without him noticing.*

Well then Gents, what's it to be? (*He listens to the orders of the imaginary crowd, nodding as he does so. Then he repeats the orders back to them, at rapid speed.*) Five pints of lager, three bitter, two whiskeys one with ice, one without, gin, gin, gin and tonic. Treble tequila, Guinness, spritzer, brown and bitter, Barbican, Budweiser, Bloody Mary, Black Velvet and a Becks, Triple X, Tiopepe, Martini, vodka and shandy and a brandy, Pernod, peanuts, crisps, crisps, crisps, crisps, crisps, crisps, crisps, two rum and okey cokey colas, and a Cherry B and cider for the groom. We'll sort that for you lads, won't we dear, (*Turns to see she's gone.*) dear, *dear!* (*Hits the bar, exits.*)

Lights up on **Mrs Iger**, *arms folded, perched on bar stool nodding to the long scream and the opening strains of Led Zeppelin's 'Whole Lotta Love'. Music suddenly stops. She speaks.*

Mrs Iger I love big men. Big quiet strong men. That's all I want. I love to tend to them. I like to have grace and flurry round them. I like their temple arms and pillar legs and synagogue chests and big mouth and teeth and tongue like an elephant's ear. And big carved faces like a naturreal cliff side, and the Roman empire bone work. And you can really dig deep into 'em, can't you? And there's so much. Gargantuan man, like a Roman Empire, with a voice he hardly uses, but when he does it's all rumbling under his breast plate. So big, big hands, big everything. Like sleeping by a mountain side. Carved men. It's a thrill if you see them run, say for a bus, pounding up the pavement. Good big man, thick blood through tubular veins, squirting and washing him out. It must be like a bloody big red cavernous car wash in there, in him, and all his organs and bits hanging from the rib roof, getting a good daily drenching in this good red blood. They are so bloody big you think they'll never die, and that's another reason you want them. Bloody ox men, Hercules, Thor, Chuck Connors, come on, bring your heads down and take from my 'ickle hand. Let me groom and coddle you. And herd you. Yes, let me gather all ye big men of our Isles and herd you up and lead you across America. You myth men. Myth men. Myth men. Big men love ya.

Little man approaches her.

Mr Iger Dear, I'm having difficulty getting to the bar again. Would you go?

Mrs Iger No. You get back in there and bring us drinks. Now.

Mr Iger I'll have another try shall I dear?

Mrs Iger No, not a try. Get them here. It's pathetic.

Mr Iger (*trying to get through the crowd*) 'Scuse . . . sorry . . .

Ow . . . Are you in the queue . . . Oh . . . Sorry . . . Could
I squeeze . . . ? No . . . Thanks . . . (*Suddenly wiping himself.*)
It's all right. It's all right. My fault . . . Whose turn is it,
do you know? . . . Well I only asked . . . (*Manages to squeeze
in to bar.*) Two please . . . Hello . . . two . . . could I . . .
'scuse . . . Here love! Ah yes, yes, could I . . . What? (*Leans
back and looks up.*) Oh yes I think you, perhaps, were first,
that's right. Please go ahead . . . Oh no, she's going to kill
me. We've been in here an hour and we've not drank yet.
It's always the same. Dear, deary me.

He suddenly notices two unattended drinks by him.

What about these two here. I couldn't. (*Looks about.*)
Could I?((*Looks about.*) I have to.

He slips off with them and back to her.

Mr Iger Here we go dear.

Mrs Iger At last. (*She takes a drink then splutters out.*) What's
this, we don't have alcoholic drinks.

Mr Iger I know, but that's all they had.

Mrs Iger You. Oh well, I'm not waiting another hour,
they'll have to do. But I must say, I must say, it is another
typical cock up by Mr Feeble man. I mean what's to
getting to a bar for a drink? Are you man or mouse?

He tries to speak.

Squeak, squeak, there's my answer. You should do
something about all this. I mean it's typical, too typical of
the little. I mean if you were big, big as I wanted, well,
well . . .

Mr Iger *suddenly cracks.*

Mr Iger (*crazed*) Right then drinks is it? Drinks. I can get
drinks. Right then. Here I go. I'm coming through. (*Barges
through to the bar.*) Straight through. I get them in, me.
Drinks. I'm the drink man. I was before everyone, me.

Everyone. (*To someone.*) Shut your face fatso. Come on now drinks, drinks, drinks for me, us, short ones, long ones . . .

As he continues raving, **Mrs Iger** *comes through.*

Mrs Iger Excuse me. Let me through. Thank you.

Mr Iger . . . I'll take all them orange ones, them green and them brown. Come on drinks here, come on, come on drinks . . .

She hits him on the back of the head, he stops.

Mrs Iger Now what's to do?

Mr Iger Drinks you wanted. I was before everyone. Drinks I say.

Mrs Iger Calm.

Mr Iger I can get drinks. I can. Oh yes.

Mrs Iger Calm.

Mr Iger Drinks I will get, will.

Mrs Iger Calm.

Mr Iger Drinks.

Mrs Iger Calm.

He goes quiet.

Mrs Iger What is it?

He's quiet.

It's me, isn't it with just too much talk of the large.

He nods.

Ay dear, what have I done to you, my dinky.

Putting her arm around him.

Mr Iger Dinky?

Mrs Iger Yes. Come here my detailed little man.

She takes him in her arms.

Your weediness is welcome here.

They separate.

Come away now. Come on. My compact chap. (*Briskly.*)
We'll do something nice, take a walk, get some fresh air.

They exit. Offstage.

Mr Iger Dear?

Mrs Iger Yes?

Mr Iger Does this mean I can sleep in the bed tonight?

Mrs Iger Don't push it.

Landlord *enters holding a bottle high.*

Landlord Here it is. Last one ever. I knew I'd seen one in
the cellar. A bloody 'Bull's eye' brown. Look at that then.
(*He undoes it.*) There you go. (*Gives it to customer.*)

Landlady *comes in, begins serving someone as soon as she enters.*

Landlady Whiskey love? Yep. (*She turns to get it.*)

Landlord (*to* **Landlady**) Hey, look who's here having a
bloody 'Bull's eye' brown.

Landlady Smelly Jimmy. Well well. We've not seen you
for years.

She continues her job of filling glass with whiskey.

How are you?

Landlord
Landlady } (*in response*) Oh we're all right.

Landlady Well I am.

She turns to serve her customer. Then, in response to something Jimmy says:

Eh. (*She drops glass, it breaks. She can't speak.*) Don't you know?

Landlord (*quickly*) Hey Jimeny, come round here mate. This side here. Come on. (*Leads him off.*) You'll remember these lot of ugly mugs won't you? (*Offstage.*) Hey, look what the cat's brought in.

Landlady (*to her customer*) Sorry love.

Gets another whiskey for them. Takes money.

Tar. Tar.

Puts it in till.

Landlady *starts kicking glass under bar.*

Landlord *enters.*

Landlord Don't do that.

He gets down picking glass up.

Landlady Why? I thought you liked things shoved out of sight.

Landlord Don't know what you mean.

Landlady You do.

Landlord *turns away, starts doing something.*

Landlady Don't you think it's funny someone should say that, tonight of all nights. Don't you?

Landlord (*picking up empty bottle off bar*) Imagine finding a bloody 'Bull's eye' brown, eh?

Landlady Don't you?

Landlord I'll save that empty as a memento.

He puts it on shelf. She grabs it and shoves it in bin.

Landlady There's already two empty mementos behind this bar.

Landlord (*turning to serve someone*) Two pints sir. One lager, one bitter.

Landlady (*behind him, penetratingly*) Don't you think it funny though someone should ask . . . Don't you?

Landlord (*puts glass under lager tap*) Lager.

Landlady Don't you? Don't you?

Landlord (*worn down, puts glass under bitter tap*) Sorry, bitter's off. I'll just go and see to that. (*Goes quickly.*)

Landlady *lifts glass of lager, gives to customer. Tries bitter tap. Laughs.*

Landlady He was wrong again. I thought as much. Look at that. Bitter's never off here dear. (*Filling glass. Looking after* **Landlord**.) Never.

Interval – if required.

Landlord *enters collecting glasses.*

Landlord Busy now, eh? You can see it busy now, eh? The hectic hour. There's been a lot of copping offs round that side, two fallings out here, and a fight, three proposals of marriage round there, and a birth in the snug. And it's nowhere near last orders yet! Not really. Not really. I always say that about this time. I like a crack with the customers now and again. Better than a crack from them, eh? Eh? So you're still here then. Glad to see it. Keep drinking that's my motto, don't stop till you drop, that's my other. Glass harvesting time now. Collect 'em in.

Collect 'em in, wish they'd bring their own. Come on, sip,
swig, and sup (*Under breath.*) ya buggers. That's right. All
right if I take your glasses love. Not the ones you're
wearing. No put them back. (*Turns to audience.*) Bloody hell.

Landlord *crosses to woman,* **Lesley,** *sitting on her own.*

Landlord Hello love, where is he tonight then?

Lesley *mumbles something.*

Landlord Hey?

Lesley *mumbles again.*

Landlord At bar?

Lesley Yeah.

Landlord (*looks round*) Looks like you've lost him then.
You'll never find him again in all that lot. Look at 'em all.
Lovely thirsty boozers. My favourites. Better get her back
and serving. (*Looks off.*) Look at her entertaining the
rabble.

Landlord *goes.*

Lesley *looks around, then looks down. Looks around, then looks
down.*

Roy *comes over with drinks.*

Roy What were he on about?

Lesley Nowt, he were just collecting glasses.

Roy Oh. Here you are. (*Puts drinks down. Sits.*) She's a
character that landlady.

Lesley She is.

They drink. Pause.

Lesley What you on?

Roy Mild.

She nods. They sit in silence.

Roy There's more strange things happen in a pub than there do on T.V. Eh?

Lesley Aye. Could I just . . . ?

Roy Bloody hell, what did your last slave die of? Bloody Hell! I've only just sat down.

Lesley No. I wanted to know if I could go to loo.

Roy 'Course you can. Okay go.

She stands up.

But don't be long.

She begins to move.

Hey, and look down.

Lesley Eh?

Roy Keep your eyes down. Every time you look up, you look at men you.

Lesley I don't.

Roy (*pointing at her*) Eh, hey, no back chat. (*Looks quickly around, making sure no one's heard him.*) Go on.

She goes.

Roy (*to someone*) Mike.

Pause.

(*To someone else.*) Sandy.

Pause.

She comes back and sits.

Roy What did you have?

Lesley Eh?

Roy What did you have, one or two?

Lesley One.

Roy You were a long time for a one.

Lesley There was someone in as well.

Roy Christ, I s'pose you got chatting.

Lesley No.

Roy No.

Lesley No.

Roy Don't 'no' me.

She edges back.

Did you say 'owt about me?

Lesley No.

Roy Who did you talk about then, someone else?

Lesley No.

Roy I told you with your no's. Who did you talk about?

Lesley We didn't even talk.

Roy Didn't even talk. Don't gi' me that. Two women in a woman's shithouse and they don't speak. You must think I'm soft. Do you?

Lesley What?

Roy Think I'm soft.

Lesley I don't know.

Roy What do you mean, don't know?

Lesley Well, I can't say no you said.

Roy Oh, if I said put your hand in the fire would you? Would you?

She shakes her head.

Roy Why not?

She looks away.

Roy No but you can talk about men in women's toilets can't you love, eh?

She keeps looking away.

If you don't answer, that means yes.

Lesley No.

Roy If you say no, two things happen: one I know you're lying, two I think about hittin' you in the face.

Lesley *looks down. He nods to someone across bar.*

Roy So, do you wanna stay here or move on?

Lesley Mmm.

Roy Christ I don't know why I bother. You've no conversation have you? Have you?

Lesley Mmm.

Roy See what I'm on about. I might as well go out with a piece of shit from that favourite woman's bog of yours, where you spent all our night.

Pause.

Do you want some more crisps?

Lesley Mmm.

Roy Well liven up then and you might get some later on. What about some 'Wotsits'?

Lesley Yes.

Roy Well there you are then. Liven up and you might get some 'Wotsits'.

Pause.

Roy They've done a nice job in here 'ant they, eh? He did a lot of it himself, knocked the snug out and everything. What's over there?

Lesley Eh?

Roy What's over there so interesting?

Lesley Nothing, I just moved me head I . . .

Roy I see. Watching the darts were you? Eh?

Lesley No I . . .

Roy What?

Lesley I don't know.

Roy Don't know. I do. See that little git in the jeans and shirt, there, him.

She looks.

Roy Okay you've seen enough now. Well I could break him like that, with my knee and my arms. Break the little wanker like that. Okay? Okay?

Lesley Okay.

Roy Would you be sad?

Lesley I don't know. I don't even know him.

Roy But you'd like to wouldn't you?

Lesley No.

Roy No. Are you sure?

She nods her head.

Roy It's just that 'okay' sounded a bit sad.

Lesley What 'okay'?

Roy That 'okay' you said before sounded a bit sad. After I'd said I'd break the little wanker. That one.

Lesley (*confused*) Oh.

Roy *stares at her a long time.*

Roy Don't make me feel small.

Lesley I'm not.

Roy I'm not having you or him or anyone making me feel small.

Lesley I'm not.

Roy Well, I just said all that then, and then felt small.

Lesley What?

Roy About him and you, and that 'okay', and you made me feel small after. When it was your fault, I said it in the first place, for looking at him.

Lesley (*beaten*) Oh.

Roy Well.

Lesley What?

Roy Are you not going to say sorry?

Lesley Sorry.

Roy Right. (*To someone across bar, raises his glass.*) Aye get 'em down yeah. Ha.

Silence.

Roy You've gone quiet. What you thinking of?

Lesley Nothing.

Roy No, no. Hold on. No. Who you thinking of?

Lesley (*pleading*) Oh Roy.

Roy No, no. When someone's quiet they're thinking, right?

Lesley Maybe.

Roy Maybe. That's a funny word to say, maybe. What you saying maybe for? That means you were. Who?

Lesley I wasn't.

Roy Who? If you wasn't, you would have said no. Who were you thinking of?

Lesley No one.

Roy Who? (*Waits.*) Who?

She shakes her head.

Roy Hey, remember what I said about no. Who?

She looks down.

Who?

She looks down more.

Who?

Lesley (*suddenly jumps up*) No one. No one at all. Can't I even have me own mind!

Roy (*embarrassed*) Sit down. Sit down.

Lesley I can't win. If I said I was thinking of every man in here naked, or I said I was thinking of you and the baby, it wouldn't make any difference. You'd still find a way of torturing me wouldn't you? Torturing! Torturing!

She storms out.

He looks round grinning, embarrassed.

Pause.

She comes back in.

Lesley I need the front door key.

Roy (*gently*) Hey, sit down love. Please sit.

She still stands.

I'm sorry. I realise what I must have done to you now. I don't know what it is. It's 'cause I care like. You know. I get carried away. Come on, sit down, please.

She does.

(*Soft.*) I didn't expect you to do that love.

Suddenly slaps her.

(*Vicious.*) You'll never do it again.

Instant blackout.

Landlord *going behind bar.*

Landlord Winding down now, winding down. We're over the top of the hill and half way down the other side. In other words the mad rush is over. So . . . (*Reaches for a glass, puts it under optics.*) Should I? Shouldn't I? Should I? Shouldn't I? Or . . . (*Puts glass under pumps.*) Should I? Shouldn't I? Should I? Or . . .

Landlady *walks in and goes straight to optics, puts her glass under. Lets measure one, two, three come out. He is watching agape. She goes and lounges against bar.*

Landlord What's going on?

Landlady Where?

Landlord Here. With your (*Mimics action.*) one, two, three. We don't do all this for nothing you know.

Landlady Ah, sod off.

Landlord How many have you had tonight anyway?

Landlady Three dray men, five regulars, a few lager louts, and the 'Cheesies' rep.

Landlord It wouldn't surprise me. It would not surprise me.

She lifts her glass in a cheers.

Landlord Come on how much? Let me smell your breath. Let me.

He goes up to her face, she turns away, he sniffs.

Landlady Don't get too close, we might accidentally kiss.

Landlord You're half sozzled, aren't you?

Landlady I'd say more than half actually.

Landlord Bloody great in'it. Bloody great.

Landlady Oh shut up.

He suddenly grabs glass off her and throws its contents down the sink. She's angry at first. Then just lounges back. Laughs.

Landlord I'd rather do that, than you have it.

Landlady Oh.

Landlord (*still looking down sink*) Yes, I would.

Landlady Oh I bet it hurt that, like throwing your blood away.

Landlord You just don't care any more do you? It may have escaped your notice, but we're trying to make a living here.

Landlady (*picking up a glass again*) This helps me to keep living here.

She goes toward optics with it. He puts his hand on hers to stop her.

Landlady Get off.

Landlord No.

Landlady Get off or I'll scream like I've been stabbed.

Landlord Do it then.

She begins to open her mouth. He lets her go. She goes to optic, gets another drink.

Landlord I'm going, I can't watch this.

Landlady What, me drinking, or your precious profits on the drip?

Landlord *doesn't look at her. He just leaves.*

She goes to drink. But can't now. Puts it down. Puts her hand over her eyes.

Blackout.

Lights up.

Fred *enters and sits.* **Alice** *enters, eating crisps, turns T.V. on, sits beside him.*

Fred Well, shall we get a drink in?

Alice I wouldn't mind so much.

Fred Well, get them in then.

Alice I will after this next programme.

Fred Okay.

Silence. She starts looking round.

Fred What you doing?

Alice I'm just looking round.

Fred You're doing counting things again.

Alice I'm not.

Fred You damn are. Do you want to go back in that white place wid' the closed doors?

Alice No fear, no.

Fred Well hang onto yourself then.

Alice I've never been the same since Elvis died.

Fred You killed him.

Alice How?

Fred By buying his records which gave him money for drugs which killed him.

Alice The King never took drugs.

Fred Not freaky drugs but slimming pills and all that, dried his blood up, constipated him. Choked his bum, he died of a choked bum.

Alice Such kingliness gone.

Fred You're fat and old.

Alice You're exactly the same.

She looks at the T.V.

Alice He's exactly the same as well.

Fred Who?

Alice Him there, behind Kirk Douglas. Very Fat.

Fred He is too. He's not going to get on that palomino horse is he?

Alice No way.

Fred He bloody is you know. You just watch.

They watch.

Alice No, they've both gone out the picture now.

Fred Do you think that's it with them now?

Alice Probably.

Fred I hope the horse comes back towards the end.

Alice It won't.

Fred What a swizz.

Silence.

Fred If I was at home I'd turn the bloody thing off.

Alice I know you would, that's why we came to the pub.

Fred Well it's not to drink that's for sure. I've only had two.

Alice Well you'll have to hang on till we're both ready.

Fred I'm ready now.

Alice Well I nearly am.

Silence.

Fred Well, what we waiting for, the film or the crisps?

Alice All the lot.

She finishes crisps: tips the packet and drains it. While he's not looking, she blows it up and pops it in his ear. They look round and start laughing.

Fred Oh ha, I don't know.

Alice Hee hee.

Fred Ha.

Suddenly points at television screen.

Fred There's the palomino again. Look at him go!

Alice I don't believe it, and the fat man too. They've gone now.

Fred I recognised him then. He was in the background in some other film we watched.

Alice I wonder if we'll see him in something else.

Fred Let's remember him, we'll give him a name.

Alice What?

Fred 'Fat-Fat'.

Alice 'Fat-Fat' what?

Fred 'Fat-Fat Palomino'.

Alice 'Fat-Fat Palomino' our favourite star.

Fred He's probably dead now, these are old pictures.

Alice Aw, I hope not.

Fred Oh, don't have the water works.

Alice I'm not. I'm not that sad about him.

Fred He was a bloody good extra though.

Alice He was.

Fred I wouldn't mind trying that.

Alice You're too fat and old.

Fred He was fat and old.

Alice Yeah, but he was a different fat and old.

Fred What do you mean?

Alice He was American-Ranch-style fat and old.

Fred What's that mean?

Alice There's different fat and olds all over the world.

Fred And what fat and old am I? English fat and old?

Alice No, sad fat, poor old.

Fred Well now I know. Anyway, you're just fat and old. Fat and old all over your little chair.

Alice We're middle-aged anyway.

Fred I know, but we look old with our fat.

They both watch tele awhile. The film ends.

Fred It's finished. Turn the tele off.

Alice Why?

Fred We turned it on.

Alice You do it.

Fred I can't with my legs.

She does. She comes back and sits.

Alice (*sings*) Are you lonesome tonight?

Fred So get them in now.

Alice (*sings*) Do you miss me tonight?

Fred Shall we get them in now?

Alice (*sings*) Are you sorry we drifted apart? (*Goes silent.*)

Fred You've gone again haven't you?

Alice It's me nerves, I can't help it.

Fred Come on, let's go home and play records.

Alice I'll cry.

Fred I'll dabble your tears.

Alice We're close in our way.

Fred Close as we can get with our fat.

Alice We've been unlucky in life but luckyish in love.

Fred Yes.

Alice Will you call me Priscilla tonight?

Fred Yes I will. (*Pause.*) Will you call me 'Fat-Fat Palomino'?

They leave. Blackout.

Landlord *enters.*

LAST ORDERS NOW. COME ON. COME ON. LAST ORDERS. LAST. LADIES AND GENTS.

Begins collecting glasses.

(*To someone in audience.*) He's had a few too many an't he love? Look at that, eh. You wanna get him home. Do you know the fireman's lift?

Last orders everybody. We've reached the point of no return. Last orders now. Come on slow throats. Last orders at the bar.

(*To someone leaving.*) Goodnight. Take care now.

(*To someone as he collects lots of glasses up.*) Did you drink all them yourself Missus? Bloody hell, you can come again you can.

He stacks them on the bar.

Any more for any more?

Last orders.

Exits.

A **Woman** *enters, slightly drunk.*

Woman (*to audience*) Are they still serving? I mustn't leave this corner for the moment. I'm the 'Other Woman', come where she shouldn't to look at my man. My man and his wife. I've not come incognito either. I've come as my bloody self; drinky, smart, a little crumpled, used to being dressed up at the wrong time in the wrong places. In the only car on a car park after dark. In strange houses in the afternoon. At bus stops in last night's make-up. And I'm not having it no, no more Mister. (*She takes out a fag, fumbles with it, drops it.*) I've come here tonight, so he can see us both. Not one in one world and one in another, but both under the same light and choose. (*As in a child's choosing rhyme.*) Ip, dip, ip, dip, ip, dip. You see this is the last time I'm going to love. I haven't got it in me to go again. So it's to be him, or it's to be something else, but not another man. No, no more. Where's that fagarette? Did I drop it? Toots to it, toots to the lot of it. Did he look then? (*She tugs at her scarf, it falls.*) He did, I'm sure. Oh Jesu! Jesu! I want him. I want to wave and scream. She

doesn't know, you know. I can tell, see, see that laugh she
makes, too free, too free by far. I think. That's how it is in
flick and shadow land, it's all thinking of others and their
movements and I am sick to the soul with it. What will he
do? What will she say? Will he come? Will he cancel? Is
that the door? Was that the car? Dare I shower? Will he
ring? Most times these wives, you know, they don't even
want them. They won't have love with them, you know.
They put them down, you know. But they won't let them
loose. My God, they will not let them loosey. And I love
loosey. Oh my God, he's coming over. Face him, face him.
No shift, shift, shift. Face him. Shift. (*She turns away.*)

Out of the dark the **Landlord** *approaches, collecting glasses. She
turns, they come face to face. Pause.*

Where is he?

Landlord Who, love?

Woman A man and his woman, they were coming this
way.

Landlord They just passed you love, and went out.

Woman Follow that couple.

She rushes after them.

Landlady (*from offstage*) Watch out love, you nearly had
me over.

Landlady Who was that?

Landlord She left her scarf.

Landlady Well, take it after her quick unless you want to
wear it.

Landlord *takes it and exits.*

Landlady *starts to put a few bottles, glasses away.*

Landlady (*to someone leaving*) Goodnight. Yeah, see you.
You do if you dare. Tara. (*To someone else.*) One for the
road is it? Okey doke. There you go love, thanks. (*To
someone at door.*) Night.

She turns back and starts: a little boy is there.

Boy Is me Dad here?

Landlady What do you say lovey?

Boy Is me Dad here?

Landlady Well I don't know love, do you want to hitch
up here and see if you can see him?

Boy *nods.* **Landlady** *lifts him up on counter.*

Landlady Can you see him?

Boy *shakes his head.*

Landlady What's his name?

Boy Frank.

Landlady Is it Frank Leigh?

Boy *nods.*

Landlady Oh, he's gone love, he left a while ago.

Boy *nods at her words, and then starts crying his eyes out.*

Landlady Oh dear, come on love, don't cry, eh?

Boy I want my Dad.

Landlady I know you do love. I know. Where've you
been?

Boy (*in sobs*) He left me outside with some pop and some
crisps and he's forgot me.

He starts crying again.

Landlady (*loving him*) Now, now, eh.

Boy I want my Dad.

Landlady Don't worry love, he'll be back. Listen now, listen. Is your Mummy at home?

Boy No, she's in hospital.

Landlady Well, I'll tell you what, if he doesn't turn up soon we'll go and find him, shall we? How's that, eh?

He seems to have calmed now. Then he suddenly starts crying again.

Landlady It's all right love. Hey, hey, come on now. I'll tell you what, let's have some more crisps shall we, while we're waiting eh?

He nods.

Landlady Okay. (*She goes behind bar.*) Let's see what we've got here. (*Suddenly she looks over and beyond him.*) Now look who I can see. Look who's just come back. (*Looking towards door.*)

Boy (*looks*) DAD! (*Tries to jump off, can't.*)

Landlady *helps him down, he almost starts to belt off.*

Landlady Hey, hey. You forgot something.

Gives him crisps. Then holds his face between her hands and kisses his forehead, lingering, looking at him, the child looking back. Then suddenly she comes round.

Go on now. Off you go.

He runs out towards his Dad. She watches him go. Then goes behind the bar. Gets a drink.

Landlord (*enters, calling back*) Hey Frank, what have I told you about kids in here? I don't know.

(*To customers.*) All right, could you drink up now. Tar. (*To* **Landlady**.) Drop the towel over the taps love.

She just turns away.

(*He takes another glass.*) Tar. (*Holds it up to look, turns it upside down, truly empty.*) You enjoyed that one didn't you. Bloody hell. Okay, see you. 'Night. Can we have your glasses please. Thank you. Tar. See you. Sleep tight.

Landlady 'Bye love.

Landlord Well that's that then. Another one over. Will you bolt up? What's up with you? Oh, I'll do it.

He goes off, hear bolts going.

He comes back in.

Landlord Come on then. (*He starts to get stuck in with the glasses.*)

Landlady Did you see that little boy?

Landlord Yeah I saw him. (*Still working.*)

Landlady Do you know what day it is today?

Landlord Yeah, another working one. Come on, let's get these lot away.

Landlady Okay. (*She puts her arm on top of counter and walks forward, all the glasses smashing to floor.*)

Landlord What you doing? OH CHRIST!

They stare at each other.

Landlady Shall I clear that side now?

She goes to do it. He grabs her.

Landlady Go on, hit me. But hit me hard.

Landlord *lets her go. He returns to work.*

Landlord I know what day it is.

Landlady Eh?

Landlord I said, I know what day it is. What do you think I am, stone?

He stops working. Looks down sink like he's going to be sick.

Landlady Seems that way.

Landlord *grabs a glass, goes to optic, lets two measures out.*

Landlady Don't.

Landlord Why not? You do.

Landlady I can stop. Oh go on, what's it to me.

Landlord That's more like it. That's nearer to it. I was getting a bit worried there, sounded like care. (*Drinks. Carries on working.*) Come on.

Landlady Eh?

Landlord Let's get going.

Landlady Is that it then? That's how you think it can go again. One little explosion, two little explosions, have a drink, carry on.

Landlord Huh. (*Working.*)

Landlady That's what's been going on for years and years. Every time we try to talk about it.

Landlord I don't know what you're on about.

Landlady You do.

Landlord Look, another time eh?

Landlady No. Not this night you don't. No slipping away. I want to talk about things.

Landlord Well I don't, okay?

Landlady You're a bastard. How the hell am I going to get this out then? How the hell am I going to get it out? I've no one to love it out of me, I've no one to knock it out of me. Just a blank man.

Landlord Tough.

She starts randomly knocking glasses off.

Landlord Don't hurt my pub!

She starts laughing.

Landlady It's not a person you know.

Landlord I know. But that's the sorry state of it. It's all I've got to care for.

Landlady Oh dear.

Landlord I hate you.

Landlady I hate you harder.

Landlord If that's the case, in these few precious hours we have to ourselves, why do we have to waste them on each other?

Landlady Because seven years ago tonight our son died . . .

There's a knock at the door. He goes out to it.

Landlord (*offstage*) No we're closed. No, no take away. No.

Bolts again. Comes back in. Continues clearing away.

Landlady I feel sick. That's the first time I've said that for almost as many years. Why did it sound corny on my lips? (*Looks up, he's not listening.*) You're not listening.

Landlord Well. (*Pause, cleaning.*) You've got to carry on. (*Pause, cleaning.*) You know that as well as I do.

She suddenly screams long, chilling and loud.

He turns to look at her, doesn't go to her, just watches until she's finished.

Then she looks up at him, like a shot animal.

Landlady I can't stand it no more! The blame hurts and burns too much.

Landlord I never blamed you.

Landlady Liar.

Landlord I did not blame you, all right?

Landlady Who did you blame then, yourself?

Landlord No.

Landlady Who did you blame then, him?

Landlord Don't say things like that!

Landlady What, leave him out of this, like he never existed, is that what you're saying?

Landlord Stop. Stop with your filth!

Landlady What? . . . You're mad.

Landlord (*back to work*) Leave the dead.

Landlady God you're worse than me.

Landlord (*working on*) I'm worse than no one, just leave it, eh?

Landlady Look we've got to get this out for our own sanity.

Landlord You worry about that, I'm all right.

Landlady It's rotted us.

Landlord Well, what's the point of bothering then?

Landlady You cold gone bastard.

Landlord Aye.

She grabs up a glass to him. He turns to her, lifts his chin.

Landlord Go on break it and shove it in where it's soft. Go on. (*Waits.*) You want to, and I don't mind.

She drops glass.

Landlady What have we come to?

She turns away.

He stays in that position, chin up.

Pause.

She turns back. She looks at him standing there like that.

Still in that position, like a statue, he speaks. Eyes closed.

Landlord I loved it when we all loved. When we all were loving. Him and . . . When we were . . . Me and you bickered like we do now, all very funny, all on the surface, but love was underneath then. Now it's hate. Hate for sure.

Silence.

Landlord *opens eyes.*

I see him every day.
My son.

Pause.

I remember when he could . . .
Pulling at the crates like his Dad.
He thought he could do it, didn't he?

I see him here like as . . .

In his pyjamas.

At night his hair was always . . . (*Touches his own head.*)
Peeping in the pub. You'd shout, but I'd always let him in, and lift him up and on the counter.

Oh God, how do you die when you're seven years old.

Covers his eyes.

Pause.

When it happened I had to turn away. I thought later I could turn back, but I couldn't. Nothing healed, it just went harder and harder and harder.

Landlady And you blamed.

Landlord No.

Landlady Liar!

Landlord No.

Landlady A blaming man. A stupid blaming man.

Landlord No.

Landlady Yes!

Landlord You were driving!

Landlady Yes!

Landlord Let's stop this.

Landlady You can't do that to me. It has to be out!

Landlord No more. (*Shakes his head.*)

Landlady Yes, all of it. We were flung. Cars in the back and side. And a over and a over. I looked at him, he was going like a rag doll, this way and that, this way and that, his little mouth wide open. Then I was gone. In the ambulance, bits I remember, some blanket round me, blood in the wool. At the hospital I remember nothing, just a black, red, black, red, like some old coal, coming and going for a very long time. When I came to I knew he'd gone. Later, one of the nurses told me. Later, you came. There were flowers everywhere. You told me you'd buried him, you said you couldn't keep his body all that time while I was in the coma. But I knew you'd done it because you blamed me.

Landlord No.

Landlady He went without my goodbye. I didn't see him in his suit and tie, in his little coffin. I saw him with his mouth wide open.

Landlord Stop.

Landlady No. No. I couldn't tell what was left between us in the hospital. But when I came home the cold set in. Really frightening cold. And we stood like strangers upstairs. And we've stood that way ever since.

He nods.

Pause.

Silence.

Landlord Please know now, I didn't blame you. And I didn't want to do that to you. But I couldn't touch anything. Please know. I had no blame. Just hard, everything hard.

Landlady Why couldn't you tell me that?

Landlord Couldn't say any . . . And from then on. All this time wouldn't talk about it, so you couldn't talk about it. I thought about it, but knew you thought I didn't. And in my quiet you thought I blamed, but I didn't. Such a lot of hurt inside. Solid. Hard.

Landlady We've held ourselves for all these years, sick of our own arms squeezing, squeezing.

They look at each other. It seems they're going to embrace. But he turns and takes a glass, and begins washing it.

Landlord In the morning, you bring his picture down and you put it up there, will you?

She nods.

They both start to clean up and put away a while, in silence.

Landlady I'll cash up tomorrow.

Landlord Aye. I'll just switch off.

He turns lights out.

In the dark.

Landlord I love you.

Landlady I love you too.

Bed

Bed was first performed at the National Theatre on
8 March 1989 with the following cast:

Captain	John Boswell
Charles	Charles Simon
Sermon Head	Graham Crowden
The Couple	Donald Bisset and Joan White
Marjorie	Margery Withers
Spinster	Vivienne Burgess
Bosom Lady	Ruth Kettlewell

Director	Julia Bardsley
Designer	Peter J. Davison
Lighting	Christopher Toulmin
Music	John Winfield

In the half light we see a bedroom with a big bed, 30ft wide or more, almost covering the stage. Up one side of the room a mountain of armchairs and a massive window and curtains. Up the other side a chest of drawers mountain and, high on the wall, a little wooden cabinet upside down.

Directly over the bed is a shelf, on which are many bedtime things covered in dust: books, bottle and spoon, broken alarm clock etc. and a thing which looks like a head or bust but is not too clear in the half dark.

We hear breathing.

Lights come up further and we are aware of seven elderly people lying in bed.

Bosom Lady I'm too warm.

Captain I'm boiling.

Charles I'm boiled.

Spinster We've all got our aches and pains.

Marjorie On the edge of sleep.

Bosom Lady Toffee eyes.

Captain I love sleeping but I can never get deep like the old days.

The Couple We share it.

Charles I suck on sleep like a boiled sweet.

Spinster Speaking of boiled, I am.

Marjorie Moon-calf. Moon-calf.

Bosom Lady Asleep in the ooze.

Bosom Lady *pulls a biscuit out of her cleavage, nibbles it.*

Charles Pass the biscuit.

Spinster Gum the crumbs.

Marjorie Mattress of bread.

Bosom Lady Well, we're all toasting it then.

Captain Speak up, I can't hear over here.

Charles No one's 'spose to, it's sleep time.

Spinster I wish I could. I wish I could. Not even a pill can help.

Marjorie Count sheep.

Captain Count sheep's arses.

Bosom Lady You old toothless dirty mouth.

Charles Shave sheep and sleep in the wool coils.

Spinster I could 'cause I always knit sleep round me.

Marjorie It is a slow thing coming I'll grant you.

Bosom Lady It takes its time.

The Couple We save sleep up.

Charles When I close my eyes, where am I? When I open them, where?

Spinster When I close my eyes, all sorts drop. When I open them after that the dark's all in pieces.

Marjorie It's like black sand when it shifts.

Bosom Lady Heavy on your chest.

Captain Pressing your breaths.

Charles I'm telepathic.

Spinster The mattress has me now.

Charles I know.

Bosom Lady Give up the ghost.

Captain (*looking under the blankets*) When you think how underwear's changed through the ages.

Charles God I wish I was under the sea, a sea sleep.

Spinster Sea-rious.

Marjorie He certainly is.

Bosom Lady My dreams are silent movies.

Captain Give us the snore song someone.

Charles I dream westerns.

The Couple We dream in time.

Spinster Who are we, where do we go?

Marjorie Cuddle me. Cuddle me.

Captain Are there refreshments.

Charles Shall we pray.

Bosom Lady (*beginning to drift off again*) Dreaming again. Folding and unfolding white again.

Charles (*going also*) A shower of feathers and snow.

Spinster (*brushes mattress as she goes*) Sugar in the bed.

They are all beginning to fall.

Bosom Lady We all lie back and just whisp away.

Back to sleep.

Long pause.

Charles *suddenly sits bolt upright.*

Charles I'm off. I put my driving hat on. (*Takes trilby out from under sheets, puts it on.*) Turn the key. Over the kerb. Nice sound underneath. Round the village pond. (*Leans into it as he goes. Waves to someone.*) Hello. Steady now over the bumps and holes. Bloody things! (*Sees someone.*) Morning Vicar. Yes splendid. Oh dear. (*Changes gear.*) Up the wee brew. Come on you can do it girl. Stop at the top.

Bosom Lady *suddenly comes up beside him with a basket on her arm.*

Bosom Lady Hello.

Charles (*surprised*) Oh.

Bosom Lady Could you just stop at the bottom shop so I can buy some strawberry jam again.

Charles Okay. But hold on tight. (*Lets brake go.*) Because here we go!

They shoot down the hill.

Bosom Lady Whoooooooooooooooooooooooo.

Charles Ha harrrrrrrrrr.

They stop at the bottom.

Bosom Lady Won't be a mo.

Charles I'll leave the engine running.

She's gone under the covers.

Captain Psss.

Charles *looks round.*

Captain It's me old boy. Going far?

Charles Could be, not sure yet.

Captain Mind if I join you?

Charles I er . . . . . .

Captain (*clinks bottles under the blankets*) I've a few fresh stout here. (*Clinks again.*)

Charles (*friendly*) Clamber in old chap, there's a rug at the back, slip them under.

He lifts **Charles'** *pillow to slip them behind.*

Captain What's this, white chicken and ham. A beautiful cheese. An apple pie.

Charles Shush. Sh. Sh.

Suddenly everyone's up and sniffing in their sleep, following their noses.

Bosom Lady (*comes back with shopping*) Strawberries, chocolate cake, spam.

At this **Marjorie** *and* **Spinster** *and* **The Couple** *clamber in on each side behind* **Charles**. **The Couple** *though sitting up remain asleep. In front,* **Captain** *is one side of* **Charles**, **Bosom Lady** *the other.*

Spinster } Are we off then?
Marjorie

Charles (*with a car full, giving in*) Oh werry vell. Werry vell.

Captain Come on the anchors away!

Spinster
Marjorie   } Yes yes.
Bosom Lady

Marjorie Foot well down. (**Charles** *presses his horn.*) PEEP
PEEP!

Spinster Wheels free.

They all shudder forward.

Marjorie We're off!

They move as though travelling. All happy.

Charles The tickle belly bridge.

They bump over it.

All Woooooooooooooo. (*Laughter.*)

Charles Down the tree lined.

They all press forward.

And out, out into the open road.

Spinster (*leans over*) Not so fast Charles. Faster!

She giggles.

Bosom Lady Yes race him. (*A passing car.*) Oh he's gone.

Charles Has he.

*He suddenly changes gear. They all make the sound of the car as
they surge forward. Wind blasted. Racing. They pass the other car.
They all cheer. Wave. Pull faces. Blow raspberries. Blow kisses. As
they pass.*

Charles (*proud*) Here we go!

At the back they begin sharing out the food and beer.

– Anyone like a

– Lovely.

– Anyone like a

– Lovely.

– Anyone.

– Lovely.

– Anyone like a.

Charles Don't forget your driver.

Bosom Lady Here we go. Chicken leg one side.

He takes a bite, as she holds it.

Marjorie Beer the other. (*She pours some in his mouth.*)

They drive and eat.

Charles Look at that. Trees and then the lake. Trees and then the lake and the sun sliced on it.

Bosom Lady Oh I love this way round.

Marjorie The sun's making the road sparkle.

Spinster You feel as though you can catch things as you pass.

Bosom Lady *makes to catch something.*

Spinster What's that?

Bosom Lady A leaf.

Marjorie *catches something.*

Spinster What's that?

Marjorie A little bird. (*Lets it go.*) There she goes.

The women all blow a kiss.

Captain *catches something.*

Spinster What's that?

Captain Some litter. (*Undoes the crumpled paper a bit.*) No a poem. England . . .

Charles *begins to say it. As he does, they all settle back down to sleep.* **Captain** *with the paper over his face.* **Charles** *continues out.*

Charles England you summer beast. You humped bridges, you singing streams, you bumble hum, you round the cottage door. England you waxy rose. You scent. You hay stem in the mouth. You peasant-backed, rich-fronted, meadows and cheese and slow turn place. England you bowler hat/crown. You English Englishness English England. You green thing. You shape. You British school of motoring. You decent breakfast. You lived in land. You and your deep green indented green covered parts. Your cities sprung and crooked and sooted and historical. Stone England. Lassie and Laddie and Lord Land. You're pinched up in places and flattened in others, you have pubs and crannies and nooks, woods and brooks, fag end and piss precincts and towns of seventies cement, and modern, the word modern. And little birds lost and coughing. And motorways strapped across the fat of your land. Dark black, lit yellow. Cars come under the lights and the bridges and inside the automobiles people's heads are buzzing, they are. There's noises that have built up over the past thirty years, new and not right and in front and behind, and the brains gone puff ball, or modernly cooked, micro chumped. Beamed. Sucky. Not to be held. Past the sell-by date. Modern man has always just eaten. He's yellowed and flabby ripe. He's useless, killable. Standing in his underpants in the middle of the motorway with a personal hi-fi on.

Charles
Captain } Screaming his bloody balls off.

Charles There's no more room in England any more for a Tra lu lu lal lal lah.

Captain *lets the paper go out the window.*

Bosom Lady I sometimes think that, and I think what a hard day's night.

They all sing the Beatles' song 'A Hard Day's Night' as they drive.

Charles Life on the open road.

Marjorie Where we going this night?

They all freeze. The lights go.

Charles You shouldn't have said night, it's gone dark now.

Bosom Lady Oh it's pitch black.

Charles Hang on. (*Makes a cluck sound with his mouth. Two of them turn on little torches under the sheet and hold them one each side as headlights.*)

They begin to travel again slowly. Slowly.

Spinster Don't go too fast down here Charles.

Bosom Lady What's that noise?

Marjorie Are there ghosts?

Captain Don't ask me, ask outside.

Bosom Lady (*looking out*) The leaves have gone black leather.

Spinster Wet too.

Marjorie It'll rain next.

Charles Watch what you say. Watch what you say.

Spinster Where are we?

Charles Is there no map?

Bosom Lady No.

Captain Yes. (*He lets the sheet crumple across his lap like a relief map and follows the folds and contours with his finger.*)

Charles We're just passing some black tucked in and shining.

Captain (*following map*) Yes yes.

Bosom Lady And a hazy dark a bit shut.

Captain (*still following the signs*) Yes yes.

Marjorie And some tall night tight, no swollen.

Captain Yes yes.

Spinster Then a corner offered. Then taken back.

Captain Yes yes.

Bosom Lady Some flittery shade.

Captain Right then! Just take the next, and there it is, a bright house of refreshment.

Marjorie Not ghosts?

Captain Not according to this.

She kisses him.

They all lean as though taking a big corner.

Charles And here we are.

To the left of them appears an area of bright light.

They go a little apprehensive again as **Charles** *stands up and walks slowly over the bed and looks into the space of light, then turns back towards them.*

Charles It's a damn disco. Come on in.

They all cross the bed and into the light, happy. They cram into the space of light. It's pleasant. They are dancing, dancing. Lights dim on them. Suddenly the head on the shelf opens its mouth and speaks.

Sermon Head
Here I am!
I'm here!
The constantly awake,
never slept,
shelved but
ever seeing,
spying my chances
with my raw eye (*Opens it wider, burning red.*)
and his partner, 'Eaten'. (*Opens other, the same.*)
To cock up your kip.
All I've got, my
eyes, mouth, spittle,
skin, all of me, 'Why not take all of me'

You wouldn't would you? Would you.
You have to.
All of me
sheds out irritation
by the night-cap full
I shed irritation all through
till dawn
and I shed it with glee
with night-twisting glee.
I savour any wakings I can cause in them.
I savour every one.
They're all that keep me
going in here, in this 'all-I've-got' head. (*Eyes shut, shaking his
head about, as though trying to get out.*)
Head! Head! Head!
Sleep doesn't want me.
Did I tell you.
Arrrrrrrrrrrrrrrrrrrrrrrrrrrrrrrrrrrhhh !
(*Half shouted, sung, at top pitch.*)
UH CHU CHU CHEE!
UH CHEE CHU CHEE CHU CHU!
UH CHU CHU CHEE!
UH CHEE CHU CHEE CHU CHU!
UH CHU CHU CHEE . . .

*This disturbs the dancers. Lights dim on him and up on dancers,
who are very disturbed now by the noise. They dance on but
uncomfortable now. The disco seems crowded. The atmosphere has
become unpleasant. They get nasty with each other. They argue
bunched tightly together moving across the bed, still in the space of
light and its boundaries, moving, the light going with them.*

Sermon Head *stops singing, his purpose accomplished. They break
and all return to bed, sitting up in bed now in a glum row. (Except*
The Couple *who have gone to sleep.) Still angry with each other.*

Throughout the following speech, they begin to doze off again.

Sermon Head As you can imagine I've made a life long
study of sleep. I've become what you might call
obsessional and snoozle fanatical. But 'tis pure academical
and leaves me still distanced from that one article, of my
desire, sleep. Oh sleep, sleep sweet roller, kiss the inside of

Sermon Head's lids and let me fall into thee. (*Closes his eyes. Opens them.*) Why not, eh? WHERE IS MY SHARE? Oh stop it Sermon Head grab yourself together. Hold your head up. Look the night right in the eye. (*He does, his eyes wide open, burning raw red.*) Look with these raging balls and sawn off sockets. Open. There. Bam. Bam.

Suddenly from sleep all of them.

All Shut up Sermon Head!

Sermon Head Oh now we have it. Here they come as usual. Sympathy, whatever happened to it? They're at me again. Taunters. Mattress yobs.

They shout. Throw things at him.

Charles Pipe down!

Sermon Head I can't wear pyjamas!

Spinster Close it!

Couple Sssssssssssh.

Sermon Head I've never stretched!

Marjorie Oh stop.

Captain Shut the trap.

Charles Quit while you're a head.

They all laugh.

Sermon Head Oh very funny.

Spinster (*mocking*) He can't ever sleep.

Sermon Head I can so. I'm just on a sleep diet that's all.

They laugh.

Sleep fats!

They ignore him.

I'll get you lot and I bloody well will. Oh yes snore on. Snore on. . . . . .

They all settle back to sleep.

I'll have a go at them. I hate them. They keep their sleep in the bank. Full vaults or overdrawn up the nostrils. Well I want 'em wakened. I wish there were more ways available to me. Wish I was a Thermostat Face, red cheek gauged. Then I could chill or could concentrate up a heat, could bake their little throats. Look at those throats all in a row like beige sausage. Like sausage rolls. Crisp up throats, crack and buckle, flake. (*He blows dust from off the shelf onto them.*)

Marjorie *gives a cough.*

Got one anyway.

Marjorie (*waking*) So thirsty oh I'm dry.

No reply.

Oh I can't sleep for it.

Captain Don't worry there. Get your head under the ocean like me.

Marjorie I'll try. So sorry all.

Spinster What is it?

Bosom Lady Her little throat keeps telling her.

Charles Halt the breath between your lips. Sip it right down then start again.

Bosom Lady Is that what you do. You genius.

Marjorie Oh so thirsty.

Bosom Lady Use your spit dear.

Sermon Head *laughs.*

Spinster Think of water.

Captain Yes sink of water.

Couple Don't mention the stuff. It makes it worse.

Charles Clunk your tongue round, there might be some juice left.

Sermon Head *laughs.*

Bosom Lady Water! Water! Water to do!

Captain I'm tucking in the waves all round, nice and cosy and splashy.

Marjorie So thirsty it's hurting.

Spinster Sssssssh you're starting me off now.

Couple Sufferings sufferings.

Sermon Head Belt up and bring her a glass of water for sleepssake!

Silence. They are all still but with eyes wide open, tense. Pause.

Couple (*slowly*) We'll go for the glass of water.

Marjorie Thank you so very much. How can I ever . . .

All of them begin pulling back the blankets and sheets industriously, busy doing their different tasks like a trained crew. The blankets are rolled back. Pillows mounted. Covers untucked. Sheets tied and knotted etc. **The Couple** *during this are putting on their dressing-gowns and slippers. The others proceed to the bed centre on all fours or knees, and ease up and ease out and ease up then suddenly out a perfect round shape of mattress, a clear lid. The slices of sheet and spring are very visible at the side like a piece of cake. And as it leaves the hole a beam of light shoots right up strong to the ceiling. They then proceed to lower* **The Couple** *down the hole by the knotted sheets. When they are out of sight they solemnly close the lid, restore the sheets etc. and silently return to bed. Then to sleep.*

Sermon Head I'm still awake. I have to mention it. You see how I had them, worried, well wakened. Staring into the light, like me. And now they're right back where we started. Sleep's too magnetic in its drawing. Won't drag me off into its dark suck though will it. Oh, you leave me so jealous! You sleep easies – You yawn friends. Slumber dogs. Doing your greed sleeping. Snoring. Lip fluttering under the covers and blankets, wool and cotton all over your mouths. Breath swopping. Look at you all in your dream wigs.

They wake.

Bosom Lady Shut up Sermon Head.

Captain Get slept.

Sermon Head Look at you in that lovely big bed, you're not worthy of it. When I think of the bed my poor Mother headed. A dirty bed. A 'kicked' bed. Squeaking in its hundred voices, the stinking square. Always moving. A corner torn off. Full of old hands and the soft sinky breasts of Victorian chars . . .

Charles Shut him up, someone.

Spinster Give him the poke.

One of them quickly pulls from under the bed a very long duster, (as long as it needs to be to reach him) sharp end first, and using this end pokes him right in the cheek with it. He starts squealing at top pitch. They poke him again. He shuts up. The duster is returned. They turn over and sleep.

Blackout.

Lights up on **The Couple,** *who are half-way up and still scaling the armchair mountain. They stop and rest in a couple of the chairs.*

Woman To

Man gether.

Woman Tied.

They kick off and the armchairs suddenly swing out and very gently go back and forth out over the bed like swings.

Woman Shared.

Man We've shared ourselves away to each other.

Woman I'd give you my air and you'd return it with yours.

Man Do we still love we.

Woman It is love but we're making it last. Are we happy?

Man I've forgotten. Did you put the cat out?

Woman Twenty years ago.

Man And it never came back the swine.

Both
One hand, one wrist, one arm. Our minds
have faded together.
Our souls are hugging.
There's only a second betwixt our hearts beats
enough just for separation.
They go
  we're two no one
    two one
  we're two no one
    two one.

Both (*sing*)
We are the kinder things of life
We place our breaths
We're in the air almost

Man We're done in watercolours.

Woman Our hearts go like rocking chairs.

Sermon Head What about the glass of water, you stupid old
sods!

They remember, park up the armchairs and hurry away.

He turns his attention to those below, still smarting from poke.

(*Whispering.*) I'll give you all sore pillows, sore pillows I will.
I'll make that a sick bed I will, I'll . . .

Someone turns over below. He goes quiet.

(*Looking at them all sleeping.*) You sod gums. You . . . Just
look at them. I hate that. They'll hate this. Well one will. (*He
starts to laugh. He gently and softly sings an old sea shanty.*)

This disturbs **Captain.** *He begins tossing and turning, thrashing
the bed-clothes. Pulling them off the others. They all pull them back.
He pulls them off. They pull them back.*

Captain (*in sleep*) No. Hold. Don't falter. Lash. Criss cross.
Send it back overboard, fill your palms with the salty stuff
and throw. Sea leave me!

He seems to settle again. Then **Sermon Head** *very softly and low* *sings a little more of the sea shanty. (Throughout this speech a great storm builds, the window blows open and a powerful gale thrashes the curtains. The others huddle in their sleep.)*

Oh not again. You blaster. I've washed tonight, I've brushed my reef. Oh no here I go. I'm up. I'm down. Hold me someone. It's raging again. The storm. All my belongings are out on the deck, travelling, like swimming sheep following each other over the side, drank away. Skidding books, wet, slapped on the wood, gone. The rains bouncing feets high. I'm going to hold on. Oh yes I am. I'm going to hold. Trapped between two ragers, the sky and the sea, hopelessly caught in the zig-zag between. We're high then low. Bouncing. Sometimes suspended a second, in so much noise it's like silence. Then flung down again. Spun and slanted by the sea. It can't bear us on its surface. There's a dead dog on the deck, *(The ladies scream, then back to sleep.)* spinning around and around in the skud, then gone. I shall hold. Oh I shall hold. It's gathering now all of it and I'm in the mid. I'm waiting. I'm holding. I'm gripping on, arms around the mast. My legs sea-logged, thrown about. I've bitten my lip off, it came away like wet paper. I'm biting my bite now. Thoughts won't stay, my mind's slid. I'm cold, numb, slub. There's my will. I can see it before my eyes. A cannon barrel. Hold. Pray hold. And you and you and you. I wish you were here now. And she, where's gone, where's gone . . . Pray from right under. Pray deep under. Pray over. Pray over. Praysa! Praysa! *(Lets out an almighty cry.)* Grarrrrrrrrrrrrrrrrrrrrrrrrrrrrrrrrrrrrrrrrrrrrrrrrrrrrrrrr! *(Suddenly, looking high and around, still standing, arms out, as though in the air. Startled, wonder-struck.)* Now I'm in a great and total circle of sea. Now thrown. But it's like flying. *(Goes down.)* Suddenly I'm in the water, supported. *(Lies down in stages.)* It's like a chair, now a plank, now wet cloth. Now my limbs are spread and free, sea-surrounded, it's hurrying to fit all my outside spaces, between my arms and body, between my legs. Warm salt waters. Lulled, passed from wave to wave. Then a seagull, the cliffs and headboard. I'm back washed up on the bed. Pillow-shored. Glad to be alive. Sea-gargled. Calm.

All their breaths and snoring become that of a calm sea off a shore.

The wind has died away. But the window is still open. **The Couple** *are perched on the window sill. Still shaken by the storm and clutching onto each other. They close the window.*

Woman (*afraid*) Oh dear.

Man Which way is it now?

Woman It's going on a long time. Are you shaking?

Man Yes I quite am.

Woman So am I.

Man I have to put your hair back it's all over the place.

He begins to do this.

Woman (*for comfort*) Bring your face close. Closer, I don't want to see it all in one go. But closer still. I want to read a little to comfort me. Our times together have turned the skin, made beautiful lines.

Man I'm still in your hair.

Woman Where did your face come from?

Man *shakes his head, still sorting her hair out.*

Woman (*she is silently going over his face, touches a mark on his skin*) Who put that there? (*Silence as she continues looking over face, closer.*) I go from one true story to another. In your smooth skin, shades, foldage and lines, I see the all of us. I . . . Closer. Close. Closer still. (*They grip tightly in an embrace.*)

Light fades off them and up on **Sermon Head.**

Sermon Head (*glares down at the sleepers*) Zedding hogs. Sleep sippers and spitters. Look at 'em cooking in their own snoring heat. One nose after another. Oh but really and truly what could be better than a night in bed. You cannot get a good English sleep these days. I can't even get a takeaway. They're not worthy of sleep them snore hogs. I am. So am. Number one sleep fan, student, swot. I've grasped all its degrees, I've got Forty Winks after me name. I've classified every type. One's sleep is well used. Another

second hand. One's is brittle. One's is see-through. One's is
alchemical. One's is passed around. One's a sleepskin rug.
One's ladling sleep from a bucket. One has the bonfire
smell. One's is bread hot. One's is very wrong. One's is clot.
One's is like hands in beautiful hair. There's all these sleep
sorts and more, oh yes more. But none come near Sermon
Head, I can't even get a thin thread of it. It's just not me.
Doesn't go with my eyes.

Stops. Then starts forming crossword words.

One down
Two, two across
Four down
Three.

Charles (*in sleep*) Three up.

Captain (*in sleep*) Two across.

Marjorie (*in sleep*) One down.

Captain How many letters?

Charles *awakes, gets his newspaper and pen out. Sits up. Starts doing
the crossword.*

Spinster (*in sleep*) Yes I'm feeling better.

Bosom Lady (*in sleep*) Are you?

Captain Two was it two?

Charles No it was five.

Marjorie Is there a 'C'?

Captain I've just been in the sea.

Bosom Lady Was it five?

Captain No, one in it?

Marjorie That's me, I'll knit. (*She awakes, gets her knitting,
Sits up.*)

Bosom Lady Who' won it?

Captain Is there an 'I' in it?

Spinster I'll iron it. (*Sits up, still in sleep. Starts smoothing pillow*)
I have to.

Charles No, there was an 'S' in it.

Bosom Lady S . . O . .

Captain I'll take four Gallions.

Charles He's back in the bloody sea.

Captain Aye aye.

Bosom Lady 'I' in it.

Spinster I am ironing it!

Bosom Lady Sure there was an 'O' in it.

Captain One or two 'O's in it. Toes in it. (*He awakes, sits up to clip his toes.*)

Charles 'C' . . .

Marjorie Who do you see?

Bosom Lady (*awakes, sitting up, looking in hand mirror*) Me.

Charles 'D' that's it
D.I.S.C.O.
Disco!

He fills it in.

Spinster awakes, stands indicating the mess the bed is in after the storm.

Spinster
Ahhh this I can no longer abide.
Neither should they.
Chaos, a roughed den in which sin can hide.
With vigour my hands shake it out.
I rawl disorder.
And I can go a choking in the thrown about.

She grabs a pile of sheets and blankets as though throttling them, and throws them straight. She continues moving over the bed, restoring it.

Even in my birth I
nipped singularly all my
Mother's side
I came out clean, not covered in blood,

a matron slide.
Since then it has always been my way,
Scouring life.
Setting standards that never stray.
(*She suddenly strokes the darkness itself.*)
The night itself I like a good black.
As from old cross or kettle
Coated back
Edwardian metal
Not too lit upon.
Rubbed or seared
to the dark of my religion.

She tries to move the blankets from **Bosom Lady** *who won't let her.*
Spinster *punches her hard in her big arm.* **Bosom Lady** *howls.*
She hits her again on the exact same spot.

Charles	Hey steady on!
Marjorie	Leave her be!
Captain	Hey!

She spins to face them arms upraised in a terrifying gesture of kill.
Hands clasped over her head, holds it, shaking shaking with anger.
Bosom Lady *moves for her. Then she brings clasped hands over to*
a kind of praying position in front of her chest, then lets them go.
And continues tidying as though nothing had happened.

Spinster
Strangely I find that in place of love, hate
is often the best
cleaning agent
to penetrate and separate.
(*Continues her work.*)
My body has kept well. Kept out of sight.
My breast bared
to no babe or light (*She touches her breasts.*)
Two sheet corners sharpened
squeezed only by age
Milkless and whitened
Bit beaten with rage.

Sermon Head Shut up you old bag!

Spinster *reaches under bed, pulls out feather duster, sharp end first.* **Sermon Head** *starts screaming. Then she turns it round to the big feathered side of the duster. He sighs with relief. She reaches up with it and briskly knocks him off the shelf. The head falls screaming to the bed. In his sleep* **Charles** *puts it under a pillow to quiet it.* **Spinster** *continues making bed.*

Spinster
This our country needs remaking
As I remake this
Its foundations are flaking
Its spirit misshapen
There's a smell rising
From where our tradition has been forsaken
It's under beds and off the shore
Putrification.
England hangs off the map
half scrounger, half whore.
Oh Britannia,
doing anything to get fat.
Morally sparse.
Fast-fingered heathens steal her crown
while mauling her arse.

She has almost finished off the tucking in. It is much too tight over them. Tucked in so tight they can hardly breathe.

As I turn back the covers
straight-lined
I also turn back my mind
to my memories, mainly
neatly stacked ashes. (*Her mood changes.*)
Save that one, the one
Where the wind over the moor dashes.
An almighty wind
Apostles in the grasses,
Cloistered trees unbound,
Sky and clod earth
shoving out the cathedral sound.
A young me there, thumping
with nature
Hymns all over my hair,
a Bible picture.

She stops herself and squeezes under tight sheets.

My life's a commandment
and in it I'm entrenched
My heart feels like a giant
silent choir clenched.
Wants to sing
after all these years,
But I've tightened it in
with ribs and fears.
Many other inner organs
are the same way gagged.
Bitterness runneth over
But love on the sharp ends
of my bigoted bones gets snagged.
(*Getting the line of the sheet under her chin just right.*)
You see I have to do my right
Keep account.
Perfect nib must be
lifted clean from page each night.
My life ledger *will be in order*
I shall not be shook off.
I have my teeth and
claws, in my God's cold shoulder.

She looks out. She looks up with just her eyes.

(*Under her breath, hard.*) Turn that light out.

Blackout.

The **Couple Man** *in a corner by himself, her slipper in his hand.
Lost.*

Man I am lost. We have got somehow separated. It's cold on
own. My breathing's gone all funny. There's dark
everywhere. (*He looks around.*) Is this loneliness? (*Pause.*)
How did I get here? I can't remember. She looked after the
memory. (*Pause.*) Was I dreaming her all these years? (*Looks
at slipper.*) Oh my dearest, I have your smell and fluff, but
you you.

Suddenly three little cries come, almost like a phone ringing. It is coming from the slipper. He puts it to his ear.

Hello.

Lights come up on **Woman**. *She has the other slipper at her ear. Talks into it.*

Woman Who is this please?

Man Is that you?

Woman Yes. Is that you?

Man Yes.

Woman Are we found?

Man We are. Are you all right, my dearest?

Woman I'm not bloody sure. Are you all right?

Man Yes. Would you care for a night stroll?

Woman Very well.

They put down the slippers and begin whistling as they walk to meet at the bed corner. She slips on her slippers then links with him. They set off pleasantly strolling.

This is a good way.

Man Yes.

Woman This corner's tricky.

Man *(agreeing)* Uh, uh.

They walk on.

Woman Are we on a sleepwalk?

Man No.

Woman Well, why aren't we in bed then?

Both *(remembering)* The glass of water!

Man It's here somewhere.

Woman There's not many places left.

They reach the drawers. They look at them. She opens bottom drawer. Searches one side.

Not in here.

He searches the other side.

Man No no.

Woman A vest. Whose is this vest?

Man (*as he moves on to next drawer*) We'll never know.

They search.

Not in here.

Woman She's depending on us.

As she passes to next drawer.

Man She is.

As he joins her at drawer.

Both We mustn't fail now.

They search.

Man Not here.

Both Where then?

Woman *looks up.* **Man** *follows the look. They see the cabinet high on the wall. They look at each other in acknowledgement.*

Man *begins to climb the drawers they have left out, as though they were a staircase.* **Woman** *holds his dressing-gown cord as he ascends. He climbs high until he reaches a level with the cabinet. He leans out and can just reach it. He manages to open it. And then things, things multitudinous come pouring, pouring out for a long, long time. It seems they will never stop. Then suddenly it is empty and we see just a glass left, but upside down on the shelf, empty, a thin light cutting through it, making it glint in its emptiness.* **Man** *reaches up for it and takes it out.*

Both Empty empty empty.

They begin to weep. This wakens **Spinster** *who gets up. She notices at the bed corner a bit of sheet sticks out; she crawls over to it, she tugs it, tugs it back, then peels it right back off the corner.*

Underneath is soft black soil. She takes from under the bed a big spade and digs into the earth, digs again. The sound wakes the sleepers, who stand and step forward in a straight line facing the audience. **Spinster** *begins to rake through the soil with her hands. She finds a small plaque on old wood. She passes it to* **Bosom Lady** *who passes it to* **Charles** *who passes it to* **Marjorie** *who passes it to* **Captain. Captain** *instantly breaks into tears at the sight of it.* **Spinster** *rakes up more, finds a little baby's shoe. She passes to* **Bosom Lady** *who passes to* **Charles** *who passes to* **Marjorie. Marjorie** *bursts into tears.* **Spinster** *rakes on, she finds a letter, she passes to* **Bosom Lady** *who passes to* **Charles** *who bursts into tears. She finds a photograph. She passes to* **Bosom Lady** *who immediately cries. She rakes more. She finds a little lace handkerchief, she begins crying herself at this, and then into it. The others gather around the patch of earth as though at a grave side and slowly let their objects fall back into the earth, still weeping.* **Spinster** *passes the handkerchief up to the others and they each dry their tears with it as she again buries the past. The hanky reaches* **Bosom Lady** *last, she dries her tears then sees* **The Couple** *are crying too and passes it up to them. They cry into it. Spinster has re-covered the earth and then, along with the others, returns to bed and sleep.* **The Couple** *cry into the handkerchief. It is so wet* **Woman** *wrings it out. It begins filling the glass. They are overjoyed. Happy. they start laughing.*

Lights fade on them.

Lights up on **Bosom Lady** *who has caught the laughter and is giggling in her sleep. She suddenly wakens and sits up laughing, throwing from under the blankets, thousands of bras of all types high into the air. They fall all over the bed.*

Bosom Lady How wonderful to just wake and bra around.

Suddenly **Sermon Head** *emerges from among the bras. One is stuck over his face and he makes a muted complaint. She sees him, removes the bra. . .*

Oh my Sermon.

. . . and kisses him passionately all over his head and face, leaving gigantic kiss marks. He is helpless in this to stop her, and screaming

at top pitch. She covers his face with her bosom. We hear his muffled screaming. She takes her bosom away; he's still screaming. She puts it back over his face.

Awww dear, look in my medicine chest.

She takes it back. He is making a different sound now as though in shock, but still moaning. **Charles** *sits up, wraps a bra around* **Sermon Head***'s face and fastens it at the back to shut him up.* **Bosom Lady** *starts kissing* **Charles.**

Charles Oh goodness gracious.

He disappears under the sheets. She turns out to the audience.

Bosom Lady In a way I am her Bosom majesty. Let me tell you, life has been just one long feather boa continually in the air! It has. If I look back along it I see one perfectly empty glass after another, and I can see in them the shimmering reflections of good food and cherries and chandeliers. I wouldn't know what 'stage' of life I am at now. But I do know when I exit through sleep, I make my entrance onto a little 'stage', lit through dusty bulbs and bedside lamps. Some nights there's a Berlin cabaret on, or a circus, a Can-Can, or my favourite, an English Music Hall, with a good all round bill of healthy entertainment.

Sermon Head *squeaks, squeaks, behind the bra. She looks round at him.*

The comedy duo!

She goes back to **Sermon Head** *and undoes bra. He is gasping in air.*
(*As a comedian.*) I say, I say, why don't you face up to it and go to the party.

Sermon Head *mouth open, shaking his head, lost.*

I s'pose it is difficult when you've no*body* to go with.

Cymbals crash.

Every one a winner, every one a gem.
Oh that crazy stage. Sand dancers, fan dancers, acrobats, then me. Doing my speciality act 'The juggling of many bras'

or giving a song, a belter, or the other kind, dedicated to
some man of mine. I take up my stance, my big armpits are
sucking in and ready for whoosh, my big fluttery hands
opening. And then there's music on the air, everywhere, a
melody under the mattress, stray notes all over the bed, then
rising, calling out to have a song flown on them.

Sings the Rogers and Hart song 'Dancing On The Ceiling'.

After the first verse **Sermon Head** *joins her in singing the rest of
the song, as they all go through a dance routine, based on sleep
movements etc. while still lying in bed. It ends. They return to sleep.*

Blackout.

Pin light on **Sermon Head.**

Sermon Head Sermon Head in bed. I've made it. But really
what a waste. Beaten, ravaged, yet still unrested. Even in
such a bed as this, sleep can resist me. I give up. I give up
everything. I give up even the trying. (*Depressed, silent.*) Wait
something's happening. My eyes they're going. Jaw too. I'm
slipping little inside. Look at me nodding. (*Head nods.*) Can,
can this be sleep at long, long last. (*As he speaks this his head is
lowering towards mattress.*)

Just as his cheek hits the delicious bed, **Captain** *lets out an
enormous snore.* **Sermon Head** *springs back upright and awake.*

No.

*Very angry now but no sound. He just bites into the sheets beside
him, then spins upstage. This causes the sheets to be tugged slightly
off the sleepers, disturbing them.*

Marjorie *stands up in a sleepwalk way. The others stand too and
link hands. As this is happening* **The Couple** *approach the bed
with the glass of tears.* **Marjorie** *leads the others around the
mattress to meet them. She stops, takes the drink, then carries on
around the mattress and back to her place with everyone holding
hands and following her in a long chain.* **The Couple** *catch on at
the end and step back onto the bed.* **Marjorie** *picks up her pillow
and crawls to sit on the extreme end of the bed holding it. The
others gather up their pillows and scatter randomly all over the bed.*

They settle to sleep, clutching their pillows.

Marjorie Oh I. Well. Yes, yes.
We'd been married only a short time by then. He went in
the morning in the evening returned. Still clean. I had it
quiet and tidy for him. The clock ticking, he read the
newspaper up in front of his face, legs crossed, dark socks
on and long ankles. I'd sit and sometimes just look at his big
shoe hanging from the ankle. And he might lower the
newspaper and look over it at me staring, and I would start
as though waking from a dream and blush. And the blush
was always a cold blush, if you know what I mean. When I
served his dinner, the laying of the plate and the cutlery
always sounded out loud on the cloth, on our wedding table
under the window. I always had my hair up in a tight bun
then. And my style of clothes were the same, same as they
are now really, same as the house, as him, as his clothes and
socks. Which I wrung out through the wringer but these
were things that he never saw. He just saw the house as it
was when he left when he returned, Hello, pulling up his
trousers at the knee, sitting, the clock tick, the cloth, the
plate, the cutlery going down into the cloth, cruet, the pale
light coming through the netted curtains. The electric light
on in winter. He never really touched me, how can I say,
properly, once when my hair was slightly falling he pushed
it back up the neck, I felt two hard fingers there, they were
there for just a second too long, then gone. The personal
part of our life was like a jolt. I would taste his pyjamas in
my mouth from his shoulder. After he'd done with me he'd
lay back sweating a little, his eyes open then squeezed shut,
he didn't let the lids drop but squeezed them shut and slept
like that all night. It was maybe that night that it happened.
I told him quietly and he nodded quietly and said he was
pleased and it would be all right. And we telephoned his
sister in Bournemouth and both told her over the phone,
and she kept saying 'How loverly, well you two, well'. But
after that it was hardly mentioned. The front door would
go. The plate would go on the table. I'd see some dust on
the radio top and think how did I miss it. He'd step in and
the newspaper and the same. But it was all right because
within all this our baby was growing. Warm inside, glowing,

and it passed up to my face and my new chubby cheeks. (*She pinches them.*) When I started it was before he went to work luckily. And he ran me to the town hospital, took me in, left for work. I remember seeing his dark head pass the one two three windows. While I stood in my coat waiting to be seen by Sister, a nice woman, but such cracked hands. And as soon as she touched me I knew something was wrong inside, it felt cold, dead, hollow as though a draught was getting in and all I could think of was his boiled ham on the plate before the vegetables were placed round it and the clean white fat on the edge and his yellow mustard across the colours, horrible yellow, almost green and the meat too pink, unnatural, and unnatural, an unnatural shape. And the baby was dead when she came out, she was gone when she came out. And when he was told he nodded and when he was told he nodded. And later at home I did this (*A gesture, like holding a baby*) and later at home I did this and after that there were no more jolts in the night and after that we spoke even less and we stayed that way. And I didn't BLOODY CARE LOVE! And though it was winter and though I was still weak I went out into the garden in the snow and I threw my wish away.

Soft white feathers begin to fall in a shower. The others awaken. They lift their faces to it. **Sermon Head** *revolves to face front.* **Captain** *flicks snow off* **Marjorie**'s *hair and shoulders. The feather fall is very heavy now.* **Charles** *puts up a big brolly; they all come underneath it. The snow feathers falling. All of them, except* **Sermon Head**, *sing a lullaby ('Loo la bye bye'). It finishes.* **Charles** *slowly brings the brolly forward and down so that it covers them all from view. On it is written —*

GOOD NIGHT

Contemporary Dramatists
include

Jean Anouilh
John Arden
Margaretta D'Arc
Peter Barnes
Sebastian Barry
Dermot Bolger
Brendan Behan
Edward Bond
Bertolt Brecht
Howard Brenton
Anthony Burgess
Simon Burke
Jim Cartwright
Caryl Churchill
Noël Coward
Lucinda Coxon
Sarah Daniels
Nick Darke
Nick Dear
Shelagh Delaney
David Edgar
David Eldridge
Dario Fo
Michael Frayn
John Godber
Paul Godfrey
David Greig
John Guare
Peter Handke
David Harrower
Jonathan Harvey
Iain Heggie
Declan Hughes
Terry Johnson
Sarah Kane
Charlotte Keatley
Barrie Keeffe
Howard Korder

Peter Barnes (three v
Sebastian Barry
Dermot Bolger
Edward Bond (six v
Howard Brenton
(two volumes)
Richard Cameron
Jim Cartwright
Caryl Churchill (two
Sarah Daniels (two v
Nick Darke
David Edgar (three v
Ben Elton
Dario Fo (two volum
Michael Frayn (three
John Godber (two vo
Paul Godfrey
John Guare
Peter Handke
Jonathan Harvey
Declan Hughes
Terry Johnson (two v
Sarah Kane
Bernard-Marie Koltè
David Lan
Bryony Lavery
Deborah Levy
Doug Lucie

Methuen World Classics
include

Jean Anouilh (two volumes)
John Arden (two volumes)
Arden & D'Arcy
Brendan Behan
Aphra Behn
Bertolt Brecht (seven volumes)
Büchner
Bulgakov
Calderón
Čapek
Anton Chekhov
Noël Coward (eight volumes)
Eduardo De Filippo
Max Frisch
John Galsworthy
Gogol
Gorky
Harley Granville Barker
   (two volumes)
Henrik Ibsen (six volumes)
Lorca (three volumes)

Marivaux
Mustapha Matura
David Mercer (two volumes)
Arthur Miller (five volumes)
Molière
Musset
Peter Nichols (two volumes)
Clifford Odets
Joe Orton
A. W. Pinero
Luigi Pirandello
Terence Rattigan
   (two volumes)
W. Somerset Maugham
   (two volumes)
August Strindberg
   (three volumes)
J. M. Synge
Ramón del Valle-Inclán
Frank Wedekind
Oscar Wilde

For a Complete Catalogue of Methuen Drama titles
write to:

Methuen Drama
215 Vauxhall Bridge Road
London SW1V 1EJ

or you can visit our website at:

www.methuen.co.uk